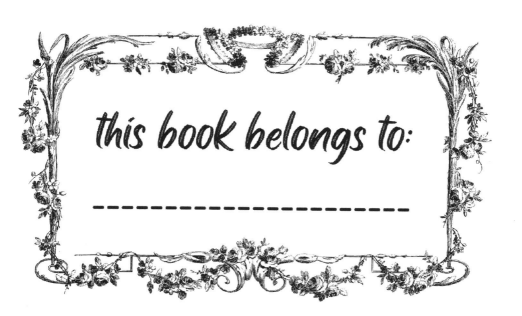

this book belongs to:

Choosing This Book
Was Truly A Great Decision.

| DATE | TIME | LOCATION |

SKETCH / SAMPLE

LENGTH	WIDTH	DEPTH

ENVIRONMENT

- ( ) FOREST
- ( ) GRASSLAND
- ( ) DESERT
- ( ) TUNDRA
- ( ) FRESHWATER
- ( ) MARINE

| TYPE | |

| SHAPE | |

| WEIGHT | |

DESCRIPTION

COLORS

TEXTURE

SETTINGS

LUSTER

EQUIPMENT

DATE	TIME	LOCATION

SKETCH / SAMPLE

LENGTH	WIDTH	DEPTH

DESCRIPTION

SETTINGS

EQUIPMENT

ENVIRONMENT

- ◯ FOREST
- ◯ GRASSLAND
- ◯ DESERT
- ◯ TUNDRA
- ◯ FRESHWATER
- ◯ MARINE

TYPE	

SHAPE	

WEIGHT	

COLORS

TEXTURE

LUSTER

DATE

TIME

LOCATION

SKETCH / SAMPLE

LENGTH	WIDTH	DEPTH

ENVIRONMENT

○ FOREST   ○ GRASSLAND

○ DESERT   ○ TUNDRA

○ FRESHWATER   ○ MARINE

TYPE

SHAPE

WEIGHT

DESCRIPTION

COLORS

TEXTURE

SETTINGS

LUSTER

EQUIPMENT

SKETCH / SAMPLE

ENVIRONMENT

- ◯ FOREST
- ◯ GRASSLAND
- ◯ DESERT
- ◯ TUNDRA
- ◯ FRESHWATER
- ◯ MARINE

TYPE

SHAPE

WEIGHT

LENGTH	WIDTH	DEPTH

DESCRIPTION

COLORS

TEXTURE

SETTINGS

LUSTER

EQUIPMENT

| DATE | TIME | LOCATION |

SKETCH / SAMPLE

LENGTH	WIDTH	DEPTH

ENVIRONMENT

- ◯ FOREST
- ◯ GRASSLAND
- ◯ DESERT
- ◯ TUNDRA
- ◯ FRESHWATER
- ◯ MARINE

TYPE	
SHAPE	
WEIGHT	

DESCRIPTION

COLORS

TEXTURE

SETTINGS

LUSTER

EQUIPMENT

| DATE | TIME | LOCATION |

SKETCH / SAMPLE

ENVIRONMENT

- ◯ FOREST
- ◯ GRASSLAND
- ◯ DESERT
- ◯ TUNDRA
- ◯ FRESHWATER
- ◯ MARINE

LENGTH	WIDTH	DEPTH

| TYPE |
| SHAPE |
| WEIGHT |

DESCRIPTION

COLORS

TEXTURE

SETTINGS

LUSTER

EQUIPMENT

DATE

TIME

LOCATION

SKETCH / SAMPLE

LENGTH	WIDTH	DEPTH

ENVIRONMENT

- ◯ FOREST
- ◯ GRASSLAND
- ◯ DESERT
- ◯ TUNDRA
- ◯ FRESHWATER
- ◯ MARINE

TYPE

SHAPE

WEIGHT

DESCRIPTION

COLORS

TEXTURE

SETTINGS

LUSTER

EQUIPMENT

DATE	TIME	LOCATION

SKETCH / SAMPLE

ENVIRONMENT

- ◯ FOREST
- ◯ GRASSLAND
- ◯ DESERT
- ◯ TUNDRA
- ◯ FRESHWATER
- ◯ MARINE

LENGTH	WIDTH	DEPTH

TYPE

SHAPE

WEIGHT

DESCRIPTION

COLORS

TEXTURE

SETTINGS

LUSTER

EQUIPMENT

DATE

TIME

LOCATION

SKETCH / SAMPLE

LENGTH	WIDTH	DEPTH

ENVIRONMENT

- ◯ FOREST
- ◯ GRASSLAND
- ◯ DESERT
- ◯ TUNDRA
- ◯ FRESHWATER
- ◯ MARINE

TYPE

SHAPE

WEIGHT

DESCRIPTION

COLORS

TEXTURE

SETTINGS

LUSTER

EQUIPMENT

DATE		TIME		LOCATION	

SKETCH / SAMPLE

ENVIRONMENT

- ◯ FOREST
- ◯ GRASSLAND
- ◯ DESERT
- ◯ TUNDRA
- ◯ FRESHWATER
- ◯ MARINE

LENGTH	WIDTH	DEPTH

TYPE

SHAPE

WEIGHT

DESCRIPTION

COLORS

TEXTURE

SETTINGS

LUSTER

EQUIPMENT

| DATE | TIME | LOCATION |

SKETCH / SAMPLE

LENGTH	WIDTH	DEPTH

ENVIRONMENT

- ◯ FOREST
- ◯ GRASSLAND
- ◯ DESERT
- ◯ TUNDRA
- ◯ FRESHWATER
- ◯ MARINE

TYPE

SHAPE

WEIGHT

DESCRIPTION

COLORS

TEXTURE

SETTINGS

LUSTER

EQUIPMENT

DATE	TIME	LOCATION

SKETCH / SAMPLE

ENVIRONMENT

- ◯ FOREST
- ◯ GRASSLAND
- ◯ DESERT
- ◯ TUNDRA
- ◯ FRESHWATER
- ◯ MARINE

LENGTH	WIDTH	DEPTH

TYPE	

SHAPE	

WEIGHT	

DESCRIPTION

COLORS

TEXTURE

SETTINGS

LUSTER

EQUIPMENT

SKETCH / SAMPLE

LENGTH	WIDTH	DEPTH

ENVIRONMENT

- ◯ FOREST
- ◯ GRASSLAND
- ◯ DESERT
- ◯ TUNDRA
- ◯ FRESHWATER
- ◯ MARINE

TYPE

SHAPE

WEIGHT

DESCRIPTION

COLORS

TEXTURE

SETTINGS

LUSTER

EQUIPMENT

| DATE | TIME | LOCATION |

SKETCH / SAMPLE

LENGTH	WIDTH	DEPTH

ENVIRONMENT

- ◯ FOREST
- ◯ GRASSLAND
- ◯ DESERT
- ◯ TUNDRA
- ◯ FRESHWATER
- ◯ MARINE

TYPE	
SHAPE	
WEIGHT	

ESCRIPTION

COLORS

TEXTURE

SETTINGS

LUSTER

EQUIPMENT

DATE **TIME** **LOCATION**

SKETCH / SAMPLE

LENGTH	WIDTH	DEPTH

ENVIRONMENT

- ◯ FOREST
- ◯ GRASSLAND
- ◯ DESERT
- ◯ TUNDRA
- ◯ FRESHWATER
- ◯ MARINE

TYPE

SHAPE

WEIGHT

DESCRIPTION

COLORS

TEXTURE

SETTINGS

LUSTER

EQUIPMENT

DATE		TIME		LOCATION	

SKETCH / SAMPLE

ENVIRONMENT

- ◯ FOREST
- ◯ GRASSLAND
- ◯ DESERT
- ◯ TUNDRA
- ◯ FRESHWATER
- ◯ MARINE

LENGTH	WIDTH	DEPTH

TYPE

SHAPE

WEIGHT

ESCRIPTION

COLORS

TEXTURE

SETTINGS

LUSTER

EQUIPMENT

DATE	TIME	LOCATION

SKETCH / SAMPLE

LENGTH	WIDTH	DEPTH

ENVIRONMENT

- ◯ FOREST
- ◯ GRASSLAND
- ◯ DESERT
- ◯ TUNDRA
- ◯ FRESHWATER
- ◯ MARINE

TYPE	

SHAPE	

WEIGHT	

DESCRIPTION

COLORS

TEXTURE

SETTINGS

LUSTER

EQUIPMENT

| DATE | TIME | LOCATION |

SKETCH / SAMPLE

LENGTH	WIDTH	DEPTH

ENVIRONMENT

- ◯ FOREST
- ◯ DESERT
- ◯ FRESHWATER
- ◯ GRASSLAND
- ◯ TUNDRA
- ◯ MARINE

TYPE

SHAPE

WEIGHT

DESCRIPTION

COLORS

TEXTURE

SETTINGS

LUSTER

EQUIPMENT

DATE		TIME		LOCATION	

SKETCH / SAMPLE

LENGTH	WIDTH	DEPTH

ENVIRONMENT

- ◯ FOREST
- ◯ GRASSLAND
- ◯ DESERT
- ◯ TUNDRA
- ◯ FRESHWATER
- ◯ MARINE

TYPE

SHAPE

WEIGHT

DESCRIPTION

COLORS

TEXTURE

SETTINGS

LUSTER

EQUIPMENT

DATE	TIME	LOCATION

SKETCH / SAMPLE

ENVIRONMENT

- ◯ FOREST
- ◯ GRASSLAND
- ◯ DESERT
- ◯ TUNDRA
- ◯ FRESHWATER
- ◯ MARINE

LENGTH	WIDTH	DEPTH

TYPE

SHAPE

WEIGHT

DESCRIPTION

COLORS

TEXTURE

SETTINGS

LUSTER

EQUIPMENT

SKETCH / SAMPLE

LENGTH	WIDTH	DEPTH

ENVIRONMENT

- ◯ FOREST
- ◯ GRASSLAND
- ◯ DESERT
- ◯ TUNDRA
- ◯ FRESHWATER
- ◯ MARINE

TYPE

SHAPE

WEIGHT

DESCRIPTION

COLORS

TEXTURE

SETTINGS

LUSTER

EQUIPMENT

DATE

TIME

LOCATION

SKETCH / SAMPLE

ENVIRONMENT

- ○ FOREST
- ○ GRASSLAND
- ○ DESERT
- ○ TUNDRA
- ○ FRESHWATER
- ○ MARINE

TYPE

SHAPE

WEIGHT

LENGTH	WIDTH	DEPTH

DESCRIPTION

COLORS

TEXTURE

SETTINGS

LUSTER

EQUIPMENT

| DATE | | TIME | | LOCATION | |

SKETCH / SAMPLE

LENGTH	WIDTH	DEPTH

ENVIRONMENT

○ FOREST   ○ GRASSLAND

○ DESERT   ○ TUNDRA

○ FRESHWATER   ○ MARINE

| TYPE | |

| SHAPE | |

| WEIGHT | |

DESCRIPTION

COLORS

TEXTURE

SETTINGS

LUSTER

EQUIPMENT

DATE	TIME	LOCATION

SKETCH / SAMPLE

ENVIRONMENT

- ◯ FOREST
- ◯ GRASSLAND
- ◯ DESERT
- ◯ TUNDRA
- ◯ FRESHWATER
- ◯ MARINE

LENGTH	WIDTH	DEPTH

TYPE

SHAPE

WEIGHT

DESCRIPTION

COLORS

TEXTURE

SETTINGS

LUSTER

EQUIPMENT

| DATE | TIME | LOCATION |

SKETCH / SAMPLE

LENGTH	WIDTH	DEPTH

ENVIRONMENT

- ◯ FOREST
- ◯ GRASSLAND
- ◯ DESERT
- ◯ TUNDRA
- ◯ FRESHWATER
- ◯ MARINE

TYPE

SHAPE

WEIGHT

DESCRIPTION

COLORS

TEXTURE

SETTINGS

LUSTER

EQUIPMENT

DATE

TIME

LOCATION

SKETCH / SAMPLE

ENVIRONMENT

- ◯ FOREST
- ◯ GRASSLAND
- ◯ DESERT
- ◯ TUNDRA
- ◯ FRESHWATER
- ◯ MARINE

LENGTH	WIDTH	DEPTH

TYPE

SHAPE

WEIGHT

DESCRIPTION

COLORS

TEXTURE

SETTINGS

LUSTER

EQUIPMENT

SKETCH / SAMPLE

ENVIRONMENT

- ◯ FOREST
- ◯ GRASSLAND
- ◯ DESERT
- ◯ TUNDRA
- ◯ FRESHWATER
- ◯ MARINE

TYPE

SHAPE

WEIGHT

LENGTH	WIDTH	DEPTH

DESCRIPTION

COLORS

TEXTURE

SETTINGS

LUSTER

EQUIPMENT

DATE	TIME	LOCATION

SKETCH / SAMPLE

ENVIRONMENT

- ◯ FOREST
- ◯ GRASSLAND
- ◯ DESERT
- ◯ TUNDRA
- ◯ FRESHWATER
- ◯ MARINE

TYPE

SHAPE

WEIGHT

LENGTH	WIDTH	DEPTH

DESCRIPTION

COLORS

TEXTURE

SETTINGS

LUSTER

EQUIPMENT

DATE		TIME		LOCATION

SKETCH / SAMPLE

LENGTH	WIDTH	DEPTH

ENVIRONMENT

- ○ FOREST
- ○ GRASSLAND
- ○ DESERT
- ○ TUNDRA
- ○ FRESHWATER
- ○ MARINE

TYPE

SHAPE

WEIGHT

DESCRIPTION

COLORS

TEXTURE

SETTINGS

LUSTER

EQUIPMENT

DATE	TIME	LOCATION

SKETCH / SAMPLE

ENVIRONMENT

- ◯ FOREST
- ◯ GRASSLAND
- ◯ DESERT
- ◯ TUNDRA
- ◯ FRESHWATER
- ◯ MARINE

LENGTH	WIDTH	DEPTH

TYPE

SHAPE

WEIGHT

DESCRIPTION

COLORS

TEXTURE

SETTINGS

LUSTER

EQUIPMENT

DATE **TIME** **LOCATION**

SKETCH / SAMPLE

ENVIRONMENT

- ◯ FOREST ◯ GRASSLAND
- ◯ DESERT ◯ TUNDRA
- ◯ FRESHWATER ◯ MARINE

TYPE

SHAPE

WEIGHT

LENGTH	WIDTH	DEPTH

DESCRIPTION

COLORS

TEXTURE

SETTINGS

LUSTER

EQUIPMENT

DATE	TIME	LOCATION

SKETCH / SAMPLE

LENGTH	WIDTH	DEPTH

DESCRIPTION

SETTINGS

EQUIPMENT

ENVIRONMENT

- ○ FOREST
- ○ GRASSLAND
- ○ DESERT
- ○ TUNDRA
- ○ FRESHWATER
- ○ MARINE

TYPE	

SHAPE	

WEIGHT	

COLORS

TEXTURE

LUSTER

DATE		TIME		LOCATION	

SKETCH / SAMPLE

LENGTH	WIDTH	DEPTH

ENVIRONMENT

- ○ FOREST
- ○ GRASSLAND
- ○ DESERT
- ○ TUNDRA
- ○ FRESHWATER
- ○ MARINE

TYPE

SHAPE

WEIGHT

DESCRIPTION

COLORS

TEXTURE

SETTINGS

LUSTER

EQUIPMENT

SKETCH / SAMPLE

LENGTH	WIDTH	DEPTH

ENVIRONMENT

- ◯ FOREST
- ◯ GRASSLAND
- ◯ DESERT
- ◯ TUNDRA
- ◯ FRESHWATER
- ◯ MARINE

TYPE

SHAPE

WEIGHT

DESCRIPTION

COLORS

TEXTURE

SETTINGS

LUSTER

EQUIPMENT

| DATE | TIME | LOCATION |

SKETCH / SAMPLE

LENGTH	WIDTH	DEPTH

ENVIRONMENT

- ◯ FOREST
- ◯ GRASSLAND
- ◯ DESERT
- ◯ TUNDRA
- ◯ FRESHWATER
- ◯ MARINE

TYPE	
SHAPE	
WEIGHT	

DESCRIPTION

COLORS

TEXTURE

SETTINGS

LUSTER

EQUIPMENT

DATE	TIME	LOCATION

SKETCH / SAMPLE

ENVIRONMENT

- ◯ FOREST
- ◯ GRASSLAND
- ◯ DESERT
- ◯ TUNDRA
- ◯ FRESHWATER
- ◯ MARINE

TYPE	
SHAPE	
WEIGHT	

LENGTH	WIDTH	DEPTH

DESCRIPTION

COLORS

TEXTURE

SETTINGS

LUSTER

EQUIPMENT

SKETCH / SAMPLE

LENGTH	WIDTH	DEPTH

ENVIRONMENT

◯ FOREST   ◯ GRASSLAND

◯ DESERT   ◯ TUNDRA

◯ FRESHWATER   ◯ MARINE

TYPE

SHAPE

WEIGHT

DESCRIPTION

COLORS

TEXTURE

SETTINGS

LUSTER

EQUIPMENT

SKETCH / SAMPLE

ENVIRONMENT

- ◯ FOREST
- ◯ GRASSLAND
- ◯ DESERT
- ◯ TUNDRA
- ◯ FRESHWATER
- ◯ MARINE

LENGTH	WIDTH	DEPTH

TYPE

SHAPE

WEIGHT

DESCRIPTION

COLORS

TEXTURE

SETTINGS

LUSTER

EQUIPMENT

| DATE | | TIME | | LOCATION | |

SKETCH / SAMPLE

LENGTH	WIDTH	DEPTH

DESCRIPTION

SETTINGS

ENVIRONMENT

- ( ) FOREST
- ( ) DESERT
- ( ) FRESHWATER
- ( ) GRASSLAND
- ( ) TUNDRA
- ( ) MARINE

| TYPE | |

| SHAPE | |

| WEIGHT | |

COLORS

TEXTURE

LUSTER

EQUIPMENT

| DATE | TIME | LOCATION |

SKETCH / SAMPLE

ENVIRONMENT

- ( ) FOREST
- ( ) GRASSLAND
- ( ) DESERT
- ( ) TUNDRA
- ( ) FRESHWATER
- ( ) MARINE

TYPE	
SHAPE	
WEIGHT	

LENGTH	WIDTH	DEPTH

DESCRIPTION

COLORS

TEXTURE

SETTINGS

LUSTER

EQUIPMENT

SKETCH / SAMPLE

LENGTH	WIDTH	DEPTH

ENVIRONMENT

- ◯ FOREST
- ◯ GRASSLAND
- ◯ DESERT
- ◯ TUNDRA
- ◯ FRESHWATER
- ◯ MARINE

TYPE

SHAPE

WEIGHT

DESCRIPTION

COLORS

TEXTURE

SETTINGS

LUSTER

EQUIPMENT

SKETCH / SAMPLE

ENVIRONMENT

- ○ FOREST
- ○ GRASSLAND
- ○ DESERT
- ○ TUNDRA
- ○ FRESHWATER
- ○ MARINE

TYPE

SHAPE

WEIGHT

LENGTH	WIDTH	DEPTH

DESCRIPTION

COLORS

TEXTURE

SETTINGS

LUSTER

EQUIPMENT

DATE

TIME

LOCATION

SKETCH / SAMPLE

LENGTH	WIDTH	DEPTH

ENVIRONMENT

- ○ FOREST
- ○ GRASSLAND
- ○ DESERT
- ○ TUNDRA
- ○ FRESHWATER
- ○ MARINE

TYPE

SHAPE

WEIGHT

DESCRIPTION

COLORS

TEXTURE

SETTINGS

LUSTER

EQUIPMENT

DATE	TIME	LOCATION

SKETCH / SAMPLE

LENGTH	WIDTH	DEPTH

ENVIRONMENT

- ○ FOREST
- ○ GRASSLAND
- ○ DESERT
- ○ TUNDRA
- ○ FRESHWATER
- ○ MARINE

TYPE	

SHAPE	

WEIGHT	

DESCRIPTION

COLORS

TEXTURE

SETTINGS

LUSTER

EQUIPMENT

DATE		TIME		LOCATION	

SKETCH / SAMPLE

LENGTH	WIDTH	DEPTH

ENVIRONMENT

- ○ FOREST
- ○ GRASSLAND
- ○ DESERT
- ○ TUNDRA
- ○ FRESHWATER
- ○ MARINE

TYPE	
SHAPE	
WEIGHT	

DESCRIPTION

COLORS

TEXTURE

SETTINGS

LUSTER

EQUIPMENT

SKETCH / SAMPLE

LENGTH	WIDTH	DEPTH

ENVIRONMENT

- ◯ FOREST ◯ GRASSLAND
- ◯ DESERT ◯ TUNDRA
- ◯ FRESHWATER ◯ MARINE

TYPE

SHAPE

WEIGHT

DESCRIPTION

COLORS

TEXTURE

SETTINGS

LUSTER

EQUIPMENT

| DATE | TIME | LOCATION |

SKETCH / SAMPLE

LENGTH	WIDTH	DEPTH

ENVIRONMENT

- ◯ FOREST
- ◯ GRASSLAND
- ◯ DESERT
- ◯ TUNDRA
- ◯ FRESHWATER
- ◯ MARINE

TYPE	
SHAPE	
WEIGHT	

DESCRIPTION

COLORS

TEXTURE

SETTINGS

LUSTER

EQUIPMENT

| DATE | TIME | LOCATION |

SKETCH / SAMPLE

ENVIRONMENT

- ◯ FOREST
- ◯ GRASSLAND
- ◯ DESERT
- ◯ TUNDRA
- ◯ FRESHWATER
- ◯ MARINE

TYPE

SHAPE

WEIGHT

LENGTH	WIDTH	DEPTH

DESCRIPTION

COLORS

TEXTURE

SETTINGS

LUSTER

EQUIPMENT

DATE	TIME	LOCATION

SKETCH / SAMPLE

LENGTH	WIDTH	DEPTH

ENVIRONMENT

- ○ FOREST
- ○ GRASSLAND
- ○ DESERT
- ○ TUNDRA
- ○ FRESHWATER
- ○ MARINE

TYPE

SHAPE

WEIGHT

DESCRIPTION

COLORS

TEXTURE

SETTINGS

LUSTER

EQUIPMENT

DATE

TIME

LOCATION

SKETCH / SAMPLE

LENGTH	WIDTH	DEPTH

ENVIRONMENT

◯ FOREST   ◯ GRASSLAND

◯ DESERT   ◯ TUNDRA

◯ FRESHWATER   ◯ MARINE

TYPE

SHAPE

WEIGHT

DESCRIPTION

COLORS

TEXTURE

SETTINGS

LUSTER

EQUIPMENT

DATE	TIME	LOCATION

SKETCH / SAMPLE

LENGTH	WIDTH	DEPTH

ENVIRONMENT

- ◯ FOREST
- ◯ GRASSLAND
- ◯ DESERT
- ◯ TUNDRA
- ◯ FRESHWATER
- ◯ MARINE

TYPE	

SHAPE	

WEIGHT	

DESCRIPTION

COLORS

TEXTURE

SETTINGS

LUSTER

EQUIPMENT

DATE

TIME

LOCATION

SKETCH / SAMPLE

ENVIRONMENT

- ◯ FOREST
- ◯ GRASSLAND
- ◯ DESERT
- ◯ TUNDRA
- ◯ FRESHWATER
- ◯ MARINE

LENGTH	WIDTH	DEPTH

TYPE

SHAPE

WEIGHT

DESCRIPTION

COLORS

TEXTURE

SETTINGS

LUSTER

EQUIPMENT

DATE		TIME		LOCATION	

SKETCH / SAMPLE

LENGTH	WIDTH	DEPTH

ENVIRONMENT

- ◯ FOREST
- ◯ GRASSLAND
- ◯ DESERT
- ◯ TUNDRA
- ◯ FRESHWATER
- ◯ MARINE

TYPE	

SHAPE	

WEIGHT	

DESCRIPTION

COLORS

TEXTURE

SETTINGS

LUSTER

EQUIPMENT

DATE

TIME

LOCATION

SKETCH / SAMPLE

ENVIRONMENT

◯ FOREST	◯ GRASSLAND
◯ DESERT	◯ TUNDRA
◯ FRESHWATER	◯ MARINE

TYPE

SHAPE

WEIGHT

LENGTH	WIDTH	DEPTH

DESCRIPTION

COLORS

TEXTURE

SETTINGS

LUSTER

EQUIPMENT

DATE

TIME

LOCATION

SKETCH / SAMPLE

LENGTH	WIDTH	DEPTH

ENVIRONMENT

- ○ FOREST
- ○ GRASSLAND
- ○ DESERT
- ○ TUNDRA
- ○ FRESHWATER
- ○ MARINE

TYPE

SHAPE

WEIGHT

DESCRIPTION

COLORS

TEXTURE

SETTINGS

LUSTER

EQUIPMENT

DATE		TIME		LOCATION	

SKETCH / SAMPLE

ENVIRONMENT

- ○ FOREST ○ GRASSLAND
- ○ DESERT ○ TUNDRA
- ○ FRESHWATER ○ MARINE

TYPE	

SHAPE	

WEIGHT	

LENGTH	WIDTH	DEPTH

DESCRIPTION

COLORS

TEXTURE

SETTINGS

LUSTER

EQUIPMENT

DATE

TIME

LOCATION

SKETCH / SAMPLE

LENGTH	WIDTH	DEPTH

ENVIRONMENT

- ◯ FOREST
- ◯ GRASSLAND
- ◯ DESERT
- ◯ TUNDRA
- ◯ FRESHWATER
- ◯ MARINE

TYPE

SHAPE

WEIGHT

DESCRIPTION

COLORS

TEXTURE

SETTINGS

LUSTER

EQUIPMENT

SKETCH / SAMPLE

LENGTH	WIDTH	DEPTH

ENVIRONMENT

- ◯ FOREST
- ◯ GRASSLAND
- ◯ DESERT
- ◯ TUNDRA
- ◯ FRESHWATER
- ◯ MARINE

TYPE

SHAPE

WEIGHT

DESCRIPTION

COLORS

TEXTURE

SETTINGS

LUSTER

EQUIPMENT

DATE **TIME** **LOCATION**

SKETCH / SAMPLE

LENGTH	WIDTH	DEPTH

ENVIRONMENT

- ○ FOREST
- ○ GRASSLAND
- ○ DESERT
- ○ TUNDRA
- ○ FRESHWATER
- ○ MARINE

TYPE

SHAPE

WEIGHT

DESCRIPTION

COLORS

TEXTURE

SETTINGS

LUSTER

EQUIPMENT

SKETCH / SAMPLE

ENVIRONMENT

- ○ FOREST
- ○ GRASSLAND
- ○ DESERT
- ○ TUNDRA
- ○ FRESHWATER
- ○ MARINE

LENGTH	WIDTH	DEPTH

TYPE

SHAPE

WEIGHT

DESCRIPTION

COLORS

TEXTURE

SETTINGS

LUSTER

EQUIPMENT

| DATE | TIME | LOCATION |

SKETCH / SAMPLE

LENGTH	WIDTH	DEPTH

ENVIRONMENT

- ◯ FOREST
- ◯ GRASSLAND
- ◯ DESERT
- ◯ TUNDRA
- ◯ FRESHWATER
- ◯ MARINE

TYPE	
SHAPE	
WEIGHT	

DESCRIPTION

COLORS

TEXTURE

SETTINGS

LUSTER

EQUIPMENT

DATE	TIME	LOCATION

SKETCH / SAMPLE

ENVIRONMENT

- ◯ FOREST
- ◯ GRASSLAND
- ◯ DESERT
- ◯ TUNDRA
- ◯ FRESHWATER
- ◯ MARINE

LENGTH	WIDTH	DEPTH

TYPE

SHAPE

WEIGHT

ESCRIPTION

COLORS

TEXTURE

SETTINGS

LUSTER

EQUIPMENT

| DATE | | TIME | | LOCATION | |

SKETCH / SAMPLE

LENGTH	WIDTH	DEPTH

ENVIRONMENT

- ◯ FOREST
- ◯ GRASSLAND
- ◯ DESERT
- ◯ TUNDRA
- ◯ FRESHWATER
- ◯ MARINE

TYPE

SHAPE

WEIGHT

DESCRIPTION

COLORS

TEXTURE

SETTINGS

LUSTER

EQUIPMENT

SKETCH / SAMPLE

ENVIRONMENT

- ◯ FOREST
- ◯ GRASSLAND
- ◯ DESERT
- ◯ TUNDRA
- ◯ FRESHWATER
- ◯ MARINE

TYPE

SHAPE

WEIGHT

LENGTH	WIDTH	DEPTH

DESCRIPTION

COLORS

TEXTURE

SETTINGS

LUSTER

EQUIPMENT

DATE		TIME		LOCATION

SKETCH / SAMPLE

LENGTH	WIDTH	DEPTH

ENVIRONMENT

- ◯ FOREST
- ◯ GRASSLAND
- ◯ DESERT
- ◯ TUNDRA
- ◯ FRESHWATER
- ◯ MARINE

TYPE

SHAPE

WEIGHT

DESCRIPTION

COLORS

TEXTURE

SETTINGS

LUSTER

EQUIPMENT

SKETCH / SAMPLE

LENGTH	WIDTH	DEPTH

ENVIRONMENT

- ◯ FOREST
- ◯ GRASSLAND
- ◯ DESERT
- ◯ TUNDRA
- ◯ FRESHWATER
- ◯ MARINE

TYPE

SHAPE

WEIGHT

DESCRIPTION

COLORS

TEXTURE

SETTINGS

LUSTER

EQUIPMENT

DATE	TIME	LOCATION

SKETCH / SAMPLE

LENGTH	WIDTH	DEPTH

ENVIRONMENT

- ◯ FOREST
- ◯ GRASSLAND
- ◯ DESERT
- ◯ TUNDRA
- ◯ FRESHWATER
- ◯ MARINE

TYPE

SHAPE

WEIGHT

DESCRIPTION

COLORS

TEXTURE

SETTINGS

LUSTER

EQUIPMENT

KETCH / SAMPLE

ENVIRONMENT

- ◯ FOREST   ◯ GRASSLAND
- ◯ DESERT   ◯ TUNDRA
- ◯ FRESHWATER   ◯ MARINE

TYPE

SHAPE

WEIGHT

LENGTH	WIDTH	DEPTH

ESCRIPTION

COLORS

TEXTURE

ETTINGS

LUSTER

QUIPMENT

DATE	TIME	LOCATION

SKETCH / SAMPLE

LENGTH	WIDTH	DEPTH

ENVIRONMENT

- ◯ FOREST
- ◯ GRASSLAND
- ◯ DESERT
- ◯ TUNDRA
- ◯ FRESHWATER
- ◯ MARINE

TYPE	

SHAPE	

WEIGHT	

DESCRIPTION

COLORS

TEXTURE

SETTINGS

LUSTER

EQUIPMENT

DATE **TIME** **LOCATION**

KETCH / SAMPLE

LENGTH	WIDTH	DEPTH

ESCRIPTION

SETTINGS

QUIPMENT

ENVIRONMENT

- ( ) FOREST   ( ) GRASSLAND
- ( ) DESERT   ( ) TUNDRA
- ( ) FRESHWATER   ( ) MARINE

TYPE

SHAPE

WEIGHT

COLORS

TEXTURE

LUSTER

SKETCH / SAMPLE

ENVIRONMENT

- ◯ FOREST   ◯ GRASSLAND
- ◯ DESERT   ◯ TUNDRA
- ◯ FRESHWATER   ◯ MARINE

TYPE

SHAPE

WEIGHT

LENGTH	WIDTH	DEPTH

DESCRIPTION

COLORS

TEXTURE

SETTINGS

LUSTER

EQUIPMENT

KETCH / SAMPLE

ENVIRONMENT

○ FOREST   ○ GRASSLAND

○ DESERT   ○ TUNDRA

○ FRESHWATER   ○ MARINE

LENGTH	WIDTH	DEPTH

TYPE

SHAPE

WEIGHT

ESCRIPTION

COLORS

TEXTURE

ETTINGS

LUSTER

QUIPMENT

DATE		TIME		LOCATION	

SKETCH / SAMPLE

LENGTH	WIDTH	DEPTH

ENVIRONMENT

- ○ FOREST
- ○ GRASSLAND
- ○ DESERT
- ○ TUNDRA
- ○ FRESHWATER
- ○ MARINE

TYPE

SHAPE

WEIGHT

DESCRIPTION

COLORS

TEXTURE

SETTINGS

LUSTER

EQUIPMENT

| DATE | | TIME | | LOCATION | |

SKETCH / SAMPLE

ENVIRONMENT

- ◯ FOREST
- ◯ GRASSLAND
- ◯ DESERT
- ◯ TUNDRA
- ◯ FRESHWATER
- ◯ MARINE

LENGTH	WIDTH	DEPTH

TYPE

SHAPE

WEIGHT

DESCRIPTION

COLORS

TEXTURE

SETTINGS

LUSTER

EQUIPMENT

DATE		TIME		LOCATION	

SKETCH / SAMPLE

ENVIRONMENT

- ◯ FOREST
- ◯ GRASSLAND
- ◯ DESERT
- ◯ TUNDRA
- ◯ FRESHWATER
- ◯ MARINE

LENGTH	WIDTH	DEPTH

TYPE

SHAPE

WEIGHT

DESCRIPTION

COLORS

TEXTURE

SETTINGS

LUSTER

EQUIPMENT

DATE

TIME

LOCATION

SKETCH / SAMPLE

LENGTH	WIDTH	DEPTH

DESCRIPTION

SETTINGS

EQUIPMENT

ENVIRONMENT

- ○ FOREST
- ○ GRASSLAND
- ○ DESERT
- ○ TUNDRA
- ○ FRESHWATER
- ○ MARINE

TYPE

SHAPE

WEIGHT

COLORS

TEXTURE

LUSTER

DATE		TIME		LOCATION	

SKETCH / SAMPLE

LENGTH	WIDTH	DEPTH

ENVIRONMENT

- ○ FOREST
- ○ GRASSLAND
- ○ DESERT
- ○ TUNDRA
- ○ FRESHWATER
- ○ MARINE

TYPE

SHAPE

WEIGHT

DESCRIPTION

COLORS

TEXTURE

SETTINGS

LUSTER

EQUIPMENT

KETCH / SAMPLE

LENGTH	WIDTH	DEPTH

ESCRIPTION

ETTINGS

QUIPMENT

ENVIRONMENT

○ FOREST   ○ GRASSLAND

○ DESERT   ○ TUNDRA

○ FRESHWATER   ○ MARINE

TYPE

SHAPE

WEIGHT

COLORS

TEXTURE

LUSTER

DATE		TIME		LOCATION	

SKETCH / SAMPLE

LENGTH	WIDTH	DEPTH

ENVIRONMENT

- ◯ FOREST
- ◯ GRASSLAND
- ◯ DESERT
- ◯ TUNDRA
- ◯ FRESHWATER
- ◯ MARINE

TYPE

SHAPE

WEIGHT

DESCRIPTION

COLORS

TEXTURE

SETTINGS

LUSTER

EQUIPMENT

DATE	TIME	LOCATION

KETCH / SAMPLE

ENVIRONMENT

- ◯ FOREST
- ◯ DESERT
- ◯ FRESHWATER
- ◯ GRASSLAND
- ◯ TUNDRA
- ◯ MARINE

LENGTH	WIDTH	DEPTH

TYPE	

SHAPE	

WEIGHT	

ESCRIPTION

COLORS

TEXTURE

ETTINGS

LUSTER

QUIPMENT

| DATE | TIME | LOCATION |

SKETCH / SAMPLE

LENGTH	WIDTH	DEPTH

ENVIRONMENT

- ◯ FOREST
- ◯ GRASSLAND
- ◯ DESERT
- ◯ TUNDRA
- ◯ FRESHWATER
- ◯ MARINE

TYPE

SHAPE

WEIGHT

DESCRIPTION

COLORS

TEXTURE

SETTINGS

LUSTER

EQUIPMENT

DATE **TIME** **LOCATION**

SKETCH / SAMPLE

ENVIRONMENT

- ◯ FOREST ◯ GRASSLAND
- ◯ DESERT ◯ TUNDRA
- ◯ FRESHWATER ◯ MARINE

TYPE

SHAPE

WEIGHT

LENGTH	WIDTH	DEPTH

DESCRIPTION

COLORS

TEXTURE

SETTINGS

LUSTER

EQUIPMENT

DATE	TIME	LOCATION

SKETCH / SAMPLE

ENVIRONMENT

- ◯ FOREST
- ◯ GRASSLAND
- ◯ DESERT
- ◯ TUNDRA
- ◯ FRESHWATER
- ◯ MARINE

LENGTH	WIDTH	DEPTH

TYPE

SHAPE

WEIGHT

DESCRIPTION

COLORS

TEXTURE

SETTINGS

LUSTER

EQUIPMENT

| DATE | TIME | LOCATION |

KETCH / SAMPLE

ENVIRONMENT

- ( ) FOREST
- ( ) GRASSLAND
- ( ) DESERT
- ( ) TUNDRA
- ( ) FRESHWATER
- ( ) MARINE

LENGTH	WIDTH	DEPTH

TYPE

SHAPE

WEIGHT

ESCRIPTION

COLORS

TEXTURE

ETTINGS

LUSTER

QUIPMENT

DATE	TIME	LOCATION

SKETCH / SAMPLE

LENGTH	WIDTH	DEPTH

ENVIRONMENT

- ( ) FOREST
- ( ) GRASSLAND
- ( ) DESERT
- ( ) TUNDRA
- ( ) FRESHWATER
- ( ) MARINE

TYPE

SHAPE

WEIGHT

DESCRIPTION

COLORS

TEXTURE

SETTINGS

LUSTER

EQUIPMENT

DATE

TIME

LOCATION

KETCH / SAMPLE

LENGTH	WIDTH	DEPTH

ESCRIPTION

ETTINGS

QUIPMENT

ENVIRONMENT

- ○ FOREST
- ○ GRASSLAND
- ○ DESERT
- ○ TUNDRA
- ○ FRESHWATER
- ○ MARINE

TYPE

SHAPE

WEIGHT

COLORS

TEXTURE

LUSTER

| DATE | TIME | LOCATION |

SKETCH / SAMPLE

LENGTH	WIDTH	DEPTH

ENVIRONMENT

- ◯ FOREST
- ◯ GRASSLAND
- ◯ DESERT
- ◯ TUNDRA
- ◯ FRESHWATER
- ◯ MARINE

TYPE

SHAPE

WEIGHT

DESCRIPTION

COLORS

TEXTURE

SETTINGS

LUSTER

EQUIPMENT

DATE	TIME	LOCATION

SKETCH / SAMPLE

ENVIRONMENT

- ◯ FOREST
- ◯ GRASSLAND
- ◯ DESERT
- ◯ TUNDRA
- ◯ FRESHWATER
- ◯ MARINE

LENGTH	WIDTH	DEPTH

TYPE

SHAPE

WEIGHT

DESCRIPTION

COLORS

TEXTURE

SETTINGS

LUSTER

EQUIPMENT

DATE	TIME	LOCATION

SKETCH / SAMPLE

ENVIRONMENT

- ◯ FOREST
- ◯ GRASSLAND
- ◯ DESERT
- ◯ TUNDRA
- ◯ FRESHWATER
- ◯ MARINE

TYPE

SHAPE

WEIGHT

LENGTH	WIDTH	DEPTH

DESCRIPTION

COLORS

TEXTURE

SETTINGS

LUSTER

EQUIPMENT

DATE

TIME

LOCATION

KETCH / SAMPLE

ENVIRONMENT

○ FOREST ○ GRASSLAND

○ DESERT ○ TUNDRA

○ FRESHWATER ○ MARINE

TYPE

SHAPE

WEIGHT

LENGTH	WIDTH	DEPTH

ESCRIPTION

COLORS

TEXTURE

ETTINGS

LUSTER

QUIPMENT

DATE		TIME		LOCATION

SKETCH / SAMPLE

LENGTH	WIDTH	DEPTH

ENVIRONMENT

- ( ) FOREST
- ( ) GRASSLAND
- ( ) DESERT
- ( ) TUNDRA
- ( ) FRESHWATER
- ( ) MARINE

TYPE

SHAPE

WEIGHT

DESCRIPTION

COLORS

TEXTURE

SETTINGS

LUSTER

EQUIPMENT

KETCH / SAMPLE

ENVIRONMENT

- ◯ FOREST
- ◯ GRASSLAND
- ◯ DESERT
- ◯ TUNDRA
- ◯ FRESHWATER
- ◯ MARINE

TYPE

SHAPE

WEIGHT

LENGTH	WIDTH	DEPTH

ESCRIPTION

COLORS

TEXTURE

SETTINGS

LUSTER

QUIPMENT

DATE	TIME	LOCATION

SKETCH / SAMPLE

ENVIRONMENT

- ◯ FOREST
- ◯ GRASSLAND
- ◯ DESERT
- ◯ TUNDRA
- ◯ FRESHWATER
- ◯ MARINE

LENGTH	WIDTH	DEPTH

TYPE	
SHAPE	
WEIGHT	

DESCRIPTION

COLORS

TEXTURE

SETTINGS

LUSTER

EQUIPMENT

KETCH / SAMPLE

ENVIRONMENT

○ FOREST   ○ GRASSLAND

○ DESERT   ○ TUNDRA

○ FRESHWATER   ○ MARINE

TYPE

SHAPE

WEIGHT

LENGTH	WIDTH	DEPTH

ESCRIPTION

COLORS

TEXTURE

ETTINGS

LUSTER

QUIPMENT

DATE	TIME	LOCATION

SKETCH / SAMPLE

LENGTH	WIDTH	DEPTH

ENVIRONMENT

- ◯ FOREST
- ◯ GRASSLAND
- ◯ DESERT
- ◯ TUNDRA
- ◯ FRESHWATER
- ◯ MARINE

TYPE

SHAPE

WEIGHT

DESCRIPTION

COLORS

TEXTURE

SETTINGS

LUSTER

EQUIPMENT

DATE **TIME** **LOCATION**

KETCH / SAMPLE

ENVIRONMENT

- ◯ FOREST ◯ GRASSLAND
- ◯ DESERT ◯ TUNDRA
- ◯ FRESHWATER ◯ MARINE

TYPE

SHAPE

WEIGHT

LENGTH	WIDTH	DEPTH

ESCRIPTION

COLORS

TEXTURE

ETTINGS

LUSTER

QUIPMENT

| DATE | TIME | LOCATION |

SKETCH / SAMPLE

LENGTH	WIDTH	DEPTH

ENVIRONMENT

- ◯ FOREST
- ◯ GRASSLAND
- ◯ DESERT
- ◯ TUNDRA
- ◯ FRESHWATER
- ◯ MARINE

TYPE

SHAPE

WEIGHT

DESCRIPTION

COLORS

TEXTURE

SETTINGS

LUSTER

EQUIPMENT

KETCH / SAMPLE

ENVIRONMENT

- ◯ FOREST
- ◯ GRASSLAND
- ◯ DESERT
- ◯ TUNDRA
- ◯ FRESHWATER
- ◯ MARINE

TYPE

SHAPE

WEIGHT

LENGTH	WIDTH	DEPTH

ESCRIPTION

COLORS

TEXTURE

ETTINGS

LUSTER

QUIPMENT

DATE		TIME		LOCATION

SKETCH / SAMPLE

ENVIRONMENT

- ◯ FOREST
- ◯ GRASSLAND
- ◯ DESERT
- ◯ TUNDRA
- ◯ FRESHWATER
- ◯ MARINE

LENGTH	WIDTH	DEPTH

TYPE

SHAPE

WEIGHT

DESCRIPTION

COLORS

TEXTURE

SETTINGS

LUSTER

EQUIPMENT

KETCH / SAMPLE

ENVIRONMENT

- ◯ FOREST
- ◯ GRASSLAND
- ◯ DESERT
- ◯ TUNDRA
- ◯ FRESHWATER
- ◯ MARINE

TYPE

SHAPE

WEIGHT

LENGTH	WIDTH	DEPTH

ESCRIPTION

COLORS

TEXTURE

ETTINGS

LUSTER

QUIPMENT

SKETCH / SAMPLE

LENGTH	WIDTH	DEPTH

ENVIRONMENT

- ◯ FOREST
- ◯ GRASSLAND
- ◯ DESERT
- ◯ TUNDRA
- ◯ FRESHWATER
- ◯ MARINE

TYPE

SHAPE

WEIGHT

DESCRIPTION

COLORS

TEXTURE

SETTINGS

LUSTER

EQUIPMENT

DATE

TIME

LOCATION

KETCH / SAMPLE

LENGTH	WIDTH	DEPTH

ESCRIPTION

ETTINGS

QUIPMENT

ENVIRONMENT

- ◯ FOREST
- ◯ GRASSLAND
- ◯ DESERT
- ◯ TUNDRA
- ◯ FRESHWATER
- ◯ MARINE

TYPE

SHAPE

WEIGHT

COLORS

TEXTURE

LUSTER

DATE	TIME	LOCATION

SKETCH / SAMPLE

ENVIRONMENT

○ FOREST　　　　○ GRASSLAND

○ DESERT　　　　○ TUNDRA

○ FRESHWATER　　○ MARINE

LENGTH	WIDTH	DEPTH

TYPE

SHAPE

WEIGHT

DESCRIPTION

COLORS

TEXTURE

SETTINGS

LUSTER

EQUIPMENT

DATE | **TIME** | **LOCATION**

KETCH / SAMPLE

ENVIRONMENT

- ◯ FOREST
- ◯ GRASSLAND
- ◯ DESERT
- ◯ TUNDRA
- ◯ FRESHWATER
- ◯ MARINE

TYPE

SHAPE

WEIGHT

LENGTH	WIDTH	DEPTH

ESCRIPTION

COLORS

TEXTURE

ETTINGS

LUSTER

QUIPMENT

DATE

TIME

LOCATION

SKETCH / SAMPLE

LENGTH	WIDTH	DEPTH

ENVIRONMENT

- ( ) FOREST
- ( ) GRASSLAND
- ( ) DESERT
- ( ) TUNDRA
- ( ) FRESHWATER
- ( ) MARINE

TYPE

SHAPE

WEIGHT

DESCRIPTION

COLORS

TEXTURE

SETTINGS

LUSTER

EQUIPMENT

| DATE | | TIME | | LOCATION | |

KETCH / SAMPLE

LENGTH	WIDTH	DEPTH

ENVIRONMENT

- ○ FOREST
- ○ GRASSLAND
- ○ DESERT
- ○ TUNDRA
- ○ FRESHWATER
- ○ MARINE

TYPE	
SHAPE	
WEIGHT	

ESCRIPTION

COLORS

TEXTURE

ETTINGS

LUSTER

QUIPMENT

DATE	TIME	LOCATION

SKETCH / SAMPLE

LENGTH	WIDTH	DEPTH

ENVIRONMENT

- ◯ FOREST
- ◯ GRASSLAND
- ◯ DESERT
- ◯ TUNDRA
- ◯ FRESHWATER
- ◯ MARINE

TYPE

SHAPE

WEIGHT

DESCRIPTION

COLORS

TEXTURE

SETTINGS

LUSTER

EQUIPMENT

DATE

TIME

LOCATION

KETCH / SAMPLE

ENVIRONMENT

○ FOREST   ○ GRASSLAND

○ DESERT   ○ TUNDRA

○ FRESHWATER   ○ MARINE

LENGTH	WIDTH	DEPTH

TYPE

SHAPE

WEIGHT

ESCRIPTION

COLORS

TEXTURE

ETTINGS

LUSTER

QUIPMENT

DATE		TIME		LOCATION	

SKETCH / SAMPLE

LENGTH	WIDTH	DEPTH

ENVIRONMENT

- ( ) FOREST
- ( ) GRASSLAND
- ( ) DESERT
- ( ) TUNDRA
- ( ) FRESHWATER
- ( ) MARINE

TYPE

SHAPE

WEIGHT

DESCRIPTION

COLORS

TEXTURE

SETTINGS

LUSTER

EQUIPMENT

DATE   **TIME**   **LOCATION**

SKETCH / SAMPLE

LENGTH	WIDTH	DEPTH

DESCRIPTION

SETTINGS

EQUIPMENT

ENVIRONMENT

- ○ FOREST   ○ GRASSLAND
- ○ DESERT   ○ TUNDRA
- ○ FRESHWATER ○ MARINE

TYPE

SHAPE

WEIGHT

COLORS

TEXTURE

LUSTER

DATE	TIME	LOCATION

SKETCH / SAMPLE

LENGTH	WIDTH	DEPTH

ENVIRONMENT

- ○ FOREST
- ○ GRASSLAND
- ○ DESERT
- ○ TUNDRA
- ○ FRESHWATER
- ○ MARINE

TYPE

SHAPE

WEIGHT

DESCRIPTION

COLORS

TEXTURE

SETTINGS

LUSTER

EQUIPMENT

DATE | **TIME** | **LOCATION**

KETCH / SAMPLE

ENVIRONMENT

- ◯ FOREST
- ◯ GRASSLAND
- ◯ DESERT
- ◯ TUNDRA
- ◯ FRESHWATER
- ◯ MARINE

TYPE

SHAPE

WEIGHT

LENGTH	WIDTH	DEPTH

SCRIPTION

COLORS

TEXTURE

ETTINGS

LUSTER

QUIPMENT

DATE		TIME		LOCATION

SKETCH / SAMPLE

LENGTH	WIDTH	DEPTH

ENVIRONMENT

- ◯ FOREST
- ◯ GRASSLAND
- ◯ DESERT
- ◯ TUNDRA
- ◯ FRESHWATER
- ◯ MARINE

TYPE

SHAPE

WEIGHT

DESCRIPTION

COLORS

TEXTURE

SETTINGS

LUSTER

EQUIPMENT

DATE | TIME | LOCATION

KETCH / SAMPLE

ENVIRONMENT

- ○ FOREST
- ○ GRASSLAND
- ○ DESERT
- ○ TUNDRA
- ○ FRESHWATER
- ○ MARINE

LENGTH	WIDTH	DEPTH

TYPE

SHAPE

WEIGHT

SCRIPTION

COLORS

TEXTURE

ETTINGS

LUSTER

QUIPMENT

DATE		TIME		LOCATION

SKETCH / SAMPLE

LENGTH	WIDTH	DEPTH

ENVIRONMENT

- ◯ FOREST
- ◯ GRASSLAND
- ◯ DESERT
- ◯ TUNDRA
- ◯ FRESHWATER
- ◯ MARINE

TYPE

SHAPE

WEIGHT

DESCRIPTION

COLORS

TEXTURE

SETTINGS

LUSTER

EQUIPMENT

DATE		TIME		LOCATION

KETCH / SAMPLE

ENVIRONMENT

○ FOREST	○ GRASSLAND
○ DESERT	○ TUNDRA
○ FRESHWATER	○ MARINE

TYPE

SHAPE

WEIGHT

LENGTH	WIDTH	DEPTH

SCRIPTION

COLORS

TEXTURE

ETTINGS

LUSTER

QUIPMENT

DATE	TIME	LOCATION

SKETCH / SAMPLE

LENGTH	WIDTH	DEPTH

DESCRIPTION

SETTINGS

EQUIPMENT

ENVIRONMENT

- ◯ FOREST
- ◯ GRASSLAND
- ◯ DESERT
- ◯ TUNDRA
- ◯ FRESHWATER
- ◯ MARINE

TYPE	

SHAPE	

WEIGHT	

COLORS

TEXTURE

LUSTER

KETCH / SAMPLE

LENGTH	WIDTH	DEPTH

ENVIRONMENT

- ◯ FOREST   ◯ GRASSLAND
- ◯ DESERT   ◯ TUNDRA
- ◯ FRESHWATER   ◯ MARINE

TYPE

SHAPE

WEIGHT

ESCRIPTION

COLORS

TEXTURE

ETTINGS

LUSTER

QUIPMENT

DATE		TIME		LOCATION

SKETCH / SAMPLE

LENGTH	WIDTH	DEPTH

ENVIRONMENT

- ◯ FOREST
- ◯ GRASSLAND
- ◯ DESERT
- ◯ TUNDRA
- ◯ FRESHWATER
- ◯ MARINE

TYPE

SHAPE

WEIGHT

DESCRIPTION

COLORS

TEXTURE

SETTINGS

LUSTER

EQUIPMENT

DATE		TIME		LOCATION

KETCH / SAMPLE

ENVIRONMENT

○ FOREST	○ GRASSLAND
○ DESERT	○ TUNDRA
○ FRESHWATER	○ MARINE

LENGTH	WIDTH	DEPTH

TYPE	

SHAPE	

WEIGHT	

:SCRIPTION

COLORS

TEXTURE

ETTINGS

LUSTER

QUIPMENT

| DATE | TIME | LOCATION |

SKETCH / SAMPLE

LENGTH	WIDTH	DEPTH

ENVIRONMENT

- ◯ FOREST
- ◯ GRASSLAND
- ◯ DESERT
- ◯ TUNDRA
- ◯ FRESHWATER
- ◯ MARINE

TYPE

SHAPE

WEIGHT

DESCRIPTION

COLORS

TEXTURE

SETTINGS

LUSTER

EQUIPMENT

DATE   TIME   LOCATION

KETCH / SAMPLE

ENVIRONMENT

◯ FOREST   ◯ GRASSLAND

◯ DESERT   ◯ TUNDRA

◯ FRESHWATER   ◯ MARINE

TYPE

SHAPE

WEIGHT

LENGTH	WIDTH	DEPTH

ESCRIPTION

COLORS

TEXTURE

ETTINGS

LUSTER

QUIPMENT

DATE	TIME	LOCATION

SKETCH / SAMPLE

ENVIRONMENT

- ○ FOREST
- ○ GRASSLAND
- ○ DESERT
- ○ TUNDRA
- ○ FRESHWATER
- ○ MARINE

LENGTH	WIDTH	DEPTH

TYPE

SHAPE

WEIGHT

DESCRIPTION

COLORS

TEXTURE

SETTINGS

LUSTER

EQUIPMENT

KETCH / SAMPLE

ENVIRONMENT

- ◯ FOREST   ◯ GRASSLAND
- ◯ DESERT   ◯ TUNDRA
- ◯ FRESHWATER ◯ MARINE

TYPE

SHAPE

WEIGHT

LENGTH	WIDTH	DEPTH

SCRIPTION

COLORS

TEXTURE

ETTINGS

LUSTER

QUIPMENT

| DATE | TIME | LOCATION |

SKETCH / SAMPLE

LENGTH	WIDTH	DEPTH

ENVIRONMENT

- ◯ FOREST
- ◯ GRASSLAND
- ◯ DESERT
- ◯ TUNDRA
- ◯ FRESHWATER
- ◯ MARINE

TYPE

SHAPE

WEIGHT

DESCRIPTION

COLORS

TEXTURE

SETTINGS

LUSTER

EQUIPMENT

DATE		TIME		LOCATION

KETCH / SAMPLE

ENVIRONMENT

- ◯ FOREST
- ◯ GRASSLAND
- ◯ DESERT
- ◯ TUNDRA
- ◯ FRESHWATER
- ◯ MARINE

TYPE

SHAPE

WEIGHT

LENGTH	WIDTH	DEPTH

SCRIPTION

COLORS

TEXTURE

ETTINGS

LUSTER

QUIPMENT

| DATE | | TIME | | LOCATION | |

SKETCH / SAMPLE

LENGTH	WIDTH	DEPTH

ENVIRONMENT

- ◯ FOREST
- ◯ GRASSLAND
- ◯ DESERT
- ◯ TUNDRA
- ◯ FRESHWATER
- ◯ MARINE

TYPE

SHAPE

WEIGHT

DESCRIPTION

COLORS

TEXTURE

SETTINGS

LUSTER

EQUIPMENT

IF YOU'RE SATISFIED WITH
MY BOOK, PLEASE GIVE ME AN
APPRECIATION OF THIS WORK.

AS A DISCERNING CUSTOMER WHO
LOVES OUR PRODUCTS, WE HAVE SOME NEW ITEMS
FOR YOU TO DISCOVER.

Just View the author.

Made in the USA
Middletown, DE
31 August 2024

60130609R00073